The Transition to Reality

Directions for Canadian Industrial Strategy

The Transition to Reality

Directions for Canadian Industrial Strategy

John J. Shepherd

Canadian Institute for Economic Policy

The opinions expressed in this study are those of the author alone and are not intended to represent those of any organization with which he may be associated.

Canadian Institute for Economic Policy
Suite 409 350 Sparks St., Ottawa K1R 7S8

Foreword

It is now widely accepted that Canada's fundamental economic problems are structural in nature; they can only be resolved by setting in place long-term policies that will permit our economic structure to adjust to the exigencies of the 'new' international economy. Correcting a serious international payments deficit, as well as imbalances in our regional economies, in our labour force and so on, will take time.

A key structural issue is the imbalance in the Canadian industrial sector that leads to massive deficits in our international balance of payments. A weak manufacturing sector led to an end-products deficit of some $17 billion in 1979, for instance, while uniquely high levels of foreign ownership of our resource and manufacturing sectors and massive borrowing abroad contributed to deficits of $6.5 billion in interest and dividends and $1.3 billion in business and other services. Regaining our ability to pay our way in the world will necessitate facing up to the causes of Canadian industrial weakness.

The Canadian Institute for Economic Policy has placed the development of a comprehensive and coherent national industrial strategy high on its study agenda. The present essay posits a framework for addressing Canada's industrial dilemma. The Institute has also commissioned specific studies of a number of key sectors and industries to buttress the policy directions outlined by John Shepherd. At present, these studies include a review of the pharmaceutical industry, industrial development related to the defence sector, industrial opportunities relative to our energy, mining and fisheries resources.

Through such studies and this suggested framework, the Institute hopes to stimulate public discussion of the directions that Canada needs to take if our national policy stances are to be consistent with the pressures of a rapidly evolving international trading environment.

Like all our authored studies, the views expressed here are those of the author, and do not necessarily reflect the views of the Institute.

R.D. Voyer
Executive Director

Introduction

The final decades of this century will witness fundamental changes in the global economic system. A multiplicity of "seismic shocks" are already affecting the existing order. They are being felt, as well, in the political and social dimensions of contemporary society.

First, the U.S. hegemony which has reigned for almost thirty years in almost all areas this side of the Iron Curtain has been fractured by fierce competition from the rest of the industrialized world. It is further threatened by new political and economic pressures from the Third World. The Viet Nam war was the most explicit indication of the United States' incapacity to single-handedly absorb the strains of empire. The more recent Afghanistan crisis reflects an environment in which the U.S. negotiates rather than dictates the Western response to the U.S.S.R. The U.S. dollar itself is subjected to the immense strains of a reserve currency in a changing world. The European Currency Unit (ECU) is being plugged into the dyke in an attempt to maintain a semblance of balance in the international monetary order.

Second, we find ourselves in transition from one dominant energy system to another, and that process is testing the foundations of Western industrial democracies. The politics of cheap oil have changed with frightening rapidity. Power has passed from the distributors and users to the producers, at a time when the West is still several decades away from achieving any politically and technically feasible commercial alternative to petroleum.

The third element of the triad of change lies in the return to slow economic growth, an abrupt reversal of the three decades of euphoric expansion after the Second World War. Stagflation is the new, puzzling and persistent force which rages and spreads as the industrialized world seeks an acceptable compromise between high economic expectations and the inevitably slower growth rate of the next ten to twenty years.

In short, the international system to which we in the West have become accustomed since World War II is de-stabilizing, with all the problems, challenges and opportunities arising from that process.

The problems now facing industrialized societies are perceived to be structural. National economies are under pressure, trading systems are changing rapidly and major displacements are under way. The rhetoric of GATT fails to mask the priority of intensified competition and proliferating non-tariff barriers.

In these unstable times, the management of change, the capacity for innovation, becomes the prerequisite for prosperity and even for survival. Greater national self-sufficiency, more effective insulation from external shock (the precursor of genuine international interdependence), is the new paradox to be resolved. Along with other nations, Canada is struggling to assess the impact of such rapid and profound change. We are striving to formulate policies for these difficult decades, policies which recognize a new world condition, and which are tailored to our own special problems and strengths.

Canada has come but recently to the acceptance and conceptualization of "industrial strategy" as a major facet of economic policy. The urgent need for policies to revitalize our industrial base was masked by the ephemeral manufacturing growth of the 1960s.

The linking of industrial health to national purpose suffered because we concentrated on distributing wealth rather than on producing it. The concept of "*an* industrial strategy" for a Canada diverse in its regions and resources was difficult to encompass. The term itself, "industrial strategy", achieved a debasement in language before acquiring a consensus as to substance. The notion of a strategy which might take one or more decades to implement does not mesh readily with the political imperatives dictated by shorter electoral time frames.

Yet the economic difficulties which Canada is encountering, and which in part we ourselves engender by lack of orchestration of policy, dictate the need for a strategic approach. A long-range and substantive attempt to revitalize our industrial base needs to be made.

Canada's belated recognition of the new realities of the international economic environment has inhibited its appreciation of recent developments in industrial policy at the international level, developments which aim both at stimulating industrial activity and at constructing new ground rules for the economic system as a whole. Consistently using the wrong language to rationalize the wrong policies, we are now doubly handicapped in a race which will de-industrialize the losers.

Semantics and Realities

In the heightened, vigorous debate over economic and industrial policy, the battle has centered upon the concepts of free trade and the free

2

market system on one side, and upon the focussed, interventionist national industrial strategies on the other. The debate itself conceals the reality. While espousing the free market economy, Western nations achieved success only when they deliberately contravened that conventional wisdom.

Indeed, the period of reconstruction after World War II rested upon the recognition that " ... left to themselves, economic forces do not work for the best, except perhaps for the powerful."[1] The re-emergence of Japan, Germany, France and other industrial nations, was stimulated and driven by conscious strategies and by concerted industrial and trading policies, resting in turn upon well orchestrated partnerships between national governments and their domestic industrial partners. The striking gains achieved by the so-called "Japanese Model" are well evidenced in the rapidly changing "value added" in manufacturing industry as shown in Chart 1.1. It is not surprising that the model has been emulated by Third World countries such as Brazil and South Korea.

Throughout the 1950s, 1960s and early 1970s, attempts at trade liberalization through the Kennedy and Tokyo Rounds of GATT were carried on in parallel with the intensified application of so-called "interventionist" policies. The central aim of these policies was to restructure national economies by building up strategic industries, while at the same time defending and shoring up the weaker, more exposed sectors. Regional development incentives, rationalization, national purchasing policies (such as are reflected by the U.S. "Buy America Act") and a wide range of tariff and non-tariff barriers were deployed to achieve this aim.

By and large, these policies for the development of industry and the stimulation of trade, to which other aspects and instruments of economic policy were subordinated, were effective—particularly in a period of almost insatiable demand. Under the regime of this "new protectionism", new patterns of trade flows and of industrial loci developed. In automobiles, petrochemicals, steel and other leading industries, countries other than the U.S. began to achieve superiority.

But, clinging to conventional wisdom, the language of the debate continued to force a polarization. A "positive" position, embracing "free trade", "free enterprise" and the "free-market" was pitted against a "negative" stance on "non-tariff barriers" and "interventionism". This polarization distorted policy development. It has also obscured the reality of a largely interventionist world. National and state purchasing policies in the heartland of U.S. "free enterprise" were, and are, as interventionist as those in France and Germany. One example is the new provisions for urban transit in the "Buy America" rules which have

CHART 1.1
DEGREE OF INDUSTRIALIZATION IN PRODUCTION AND EXPORTS
1955 and 1970

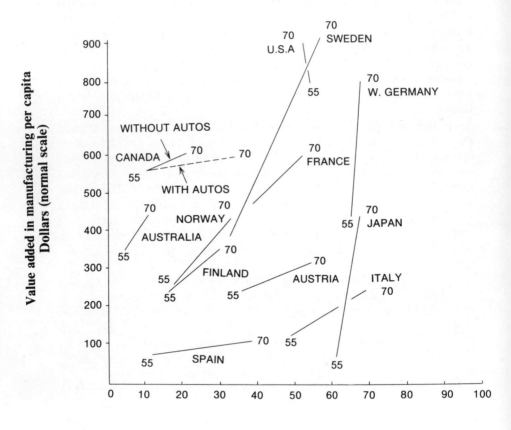

FINISHED MANUFACTURES
(per cent of total exports)

Source: *Uncertain Prospects: Canadian Manufacturing Industry 1971-77;* Science Council of Canada, October 1977.

4

given preference to U.S. firms unless foreign companies provide 51 per cent U.S. content in components and final assembly in the U.S. These provisions impact on the Canadian potential to sell $199 million in rail transit to the U.S. between 1981 and 1985, rising to $439 million between 1986 and 1990[2]. It is as fruitless to tender from countries outside the U.S. on a major weapon system as it is to seek a large communications system contract in Japan. Tax and other incentives for an auto-plant are as substantial in the United States as they are in Italy. The European Economic Community is no exception.

The protectionist "Europe first" attitude of European governments has a direct impact on Canada's ability to sell its products abroad. W. Ross DeGeer, Ontario Agent-General, expressed concern to the Trilateral Commission about developing a successful export trade to Europe:

> One of the worrying features of trade and investment relations with Europe is that a wide range of potential manufactured exports from Canada, and particularly from Ontario, are in products where the potential European buyers are in the government-controlled sector ... DeGeer said he sees great opportunities in Europe for specialized Canadian-made products in the urban transportation, telecommunications, energy generation and transmission sectors. However, . . . the markets for these products are government-procurement markets where European producers are protected by tariffs and buy-national policies, giving them almost infinite protection in their domestic markets against Canadian competition.[3]

Each and every country, therefore, has evolved its own arsenal of imaginative non-tariff barriers, whether they be disincentives to foreign corporations desiring access to the domestic market, or direct incentives to domestic industry to replace imports and to increase exports.

As departures from the conventional wisdom have become more evident, new language has been deployed to obfuscate the trend and to hide the reality of substantive change. Import restrictions are described as "voluntary quotas". "Free trade" has been unsubtly transposed to "free trade with ground rules", or to "fair trade". "Organized free trade" is perhaps the ultimate absurdity.

More fundamentally, however, these semantic difficulties may reflect the beginning of an attempt to find a new language, and a new set of ground rules, for a new world of fierce trading rivalries, of competitive industrial policies, of widespread economic restructuring. It is clear that such a language and such ground rules are urgently needed. "Interventionist" policies are not only desirable, they are palpably inescapable. The evidence, in the Netherlands with regard to shipbuilding, in Britain in microprocessors and in France in communications, is visible and overt. Rather than continuing to decry and resist such

5

policies abroad, while subscribing to them at home under appropriate euphemisms, we, as an industrial economy, have to design a new industrial strategy which will integrate with our national economic objectives, which will build national strength, and which at the same time will contribute to global economic benefit.

In recent months, both the OECD[4] (see Appendix) and the Trilateral Commission[5] have responded to the need to provide a framework for interventionist industrial strategies. In its commissioned 1979 paper on industrial policy and the international economy, the Trilateral Commission sets out to create a positive synthesis between the free market system and national industrial policies:

> Industrial policy should be coordinated with other branches of structural policy . . . industrial policies can, to be sure, lead to waste, inefficiency and protectionism . . . but our approach, while taking full account of social needs, differs dramatically from a concept of industrial policy that amounts to defensive interventionism. A sound industrial policy must recognize that the enterprise sector is the prime mover in the economy. Its premise is that market forces and entrepreneurship are the foundation of the economic system . . . It works with them and not against them . . . In this way, public policy can help to strengthen industry and facilitate the structural transformation of the economy. It can contain or weed out the economic and social measures that reduce the dynamism of industry, and smooth the way toward an economy that is more skill-intensive, science-based and high in value added. Positive industrial policies can promote innovation, research, development, investment and the establishment of new firms; and this can be linked with manpower policies that ensure training for the necessary skills. Industrial policy can also buy timing for infant or declining sectors.[6]

Within this statement, all the cardinal elements of what have previously been categorized as the "new protectionism" have been mandated, and this by an institution, the Trilateral Commission, noted for its commitment to the ethos of industrial competitiveness. The support of infant industries, defensive strategies for declining sectors, specialization, discretionary incentives for science-based activity, rationalization all become valid, provided that they meet the test of contributing to the strengthening of "market forces and entrepreneurship". At a stroke, the industrial strategies of Japan, Germany, France, Sweden, the Netherlands, in all their awesome variety, are legitimized under the rubric of "positive adjustment policies".

Yet the criterion of contributing to the strengthening of market forces and entrepreneurship is important as a foundation for a new approach to industrial policy. Although as yet lacking in rigour, it can serve as a starting point for new, more detailed guidelines for positive industrial policies, whose aim is to strengthen the national industrial base in order to meet the test of the competitive international marketplace.

It may well be that Canada, as a nation whose trading activity represents some 25 per cent of its GNP, and as a country uncommitted to any major trading bloc, could play an important part in developing such guidelines, in bringing order to the trading jungle. An international initiative in this direction, from Canada, would be welcome. But such an initiative could only emerge, and could only be credible, when we have understood the environment, mastered the language and developed the muscle to compete. Losers do not dictate change. In the meantime, Canadians have to survive and prosper in the "interventionist" world. We have to develop, with skill and vigour and urgency, the positive adjustment policies which will strengthen our own industrial base to high levels of competitive excellence. Both philosophically and practically, the climate is now favourable to that endeavour. The transition to reality is in train, and Canada must hasten to commit itself.

The need for such a commitment is already being articulated in the United States:

> A national industrial policy should and could strengthen the best in us; it can mobilize our innovative genius and ultimately free us from playing without a team strategy in a crucial game in which the other players know exactly what they want to do—and how they plan to do it.[7]

We, in Canada, would do well to heed this message. A Canadian industrial strategy is vital, feasible and long overdue.

An Industrial Strategy for Canada

Industrial strategies cannot successfully be imported without adaptation to local circumstances. The strengths, weaknesses and opportunities confronting each nation impose widely disparate needs and methods. Institutional characteristics vary greatly. The conduits and modalities of policy formulation shape and influence the policies most appropriate to each national circumstance. A Japan with no domestic conventional energy resource, and equipped with an integrated managerial system, will evolve a unique kind of industrial strategy. A Germany with a relatively powerful industrial sector will evolve its own special brand of policy. Each industrial economy will fashion its own dynamic comparative advantage with its special economic characteristics and market position in mind.

Canada is a huge, Northern, resource-producing country with a small, highly-skilled population which has high expectations as to standards of living. Our insistence on independence and national sovereignty, in defiance of economic geography, has been the formative influence behind the "National Policy". The railways, the national communications network, satellites, the provincial hydros, the banking system, are all reflections of a collective Canadian determination to enhance our sovereignty.

Now, in the face of changing external and internal pressures, and recognizing our stage of development, we have to move forward more rapidly, remoulding our industrial policy framework and re-energizing our productive capacity. As the merchandise trading balance indicates (see Chart 1.2), the heart of that problem is the chronic weakness of our manufacturing (end products) sector and an industrial strategy for Canada must primarily address that problem. The challenge is to create a broader, revitalized manufacturing activity, regionally balanced and stressing technological advance. An economy based on a "central-Canadian manufacturing system", itself relying upon the large scale importation of obsolescent production technology, will no longer suffice. Managerial autonomy and domestic investment in domestic enterprise are imperatives which will have to be recognized. Integrating the resource and the manufacturing economies in Canada is of paramount importance.

These and other factors dictate a new appraisal of our industrial policies not only in content, but with more emphasis than before on their coherence.

The "system architecture" of a Canadian industrial strategy focussed on revitalizing the manufacturing sector, embraces the following cardinal elements:

1. The need to subordinate monetary policy and other facets of economic strategy to industrial and trading imperatives.
2. The linking of the resource base to the secondary manufacturing sector.
3. A rapid increase in industrial productivity through capital and technology investment.
4. An increase in the "birth rate" of new innovative enterprises.
5. An increase in the domestic ownership and control of industry.
6. The optimization of the Canadian common market.
7. The adoption of positive, discretionary policies for
   — attacking the newer, broad fronts of research which will determine the pace and direction of future economic growth;
   — capitalizing on the technology fronts which show great commercial opportunity.

CHART 1.2
MERCHANDISE TRADE BALANCE

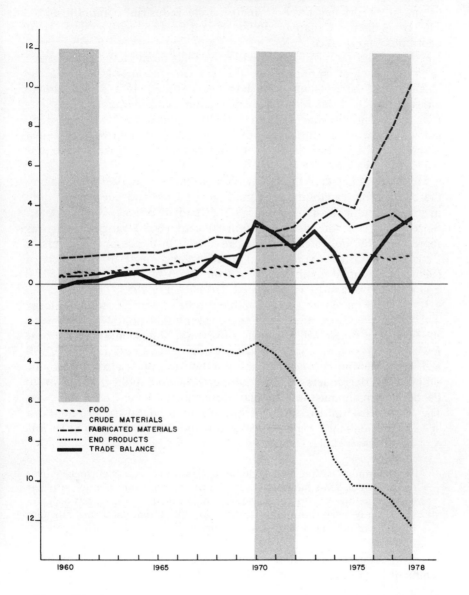

Source: H.L. Robinson, *Canada's Crippled Dollar,* Canadian Institute for Economic Policy, 1980, p. 57.

9

1. Monetary Policy and Economic Strategy

In Canada, we have not paid enough attention to the importance of comparative currency levels in maintaining industrial competitiveness. The swing in the Canadian dollar from 1.04 U.S. to 0.85 U.S. is of enormous significance compared to any level of tariff adjustment emerging from the GATT negotiations. What manufacturing competitiveness we enjoy springs from the current, favourable rate of exchange. Yet the exchange rate has been treated as a policy almost entirely distinct from industrial and trading considerations. Mesmerized by the notion that economic health equates with 100 cent U.S. par value, we have consistently defended the Canadian dollar against a fall to its realistic, productivity determined value, and have applauded its rise toward parity.

Monetary policy kept the dollar high (from 1972 to 1976),[8] damaging the competitive capability of Canadian industry and succeeding only in deferring a substantial decline which had to occur sooner or later. Since 1978, it is the dollar in mid-80 cent (U.S.) range which has represented the only significant improvement in the competitiveness of Canadian industry. Even with that advantage our trading deficit in fully manufactured goods has risen from $12.3 billion in 1978 to $17.0 billion in 1979,[9] and to an estimated $18 billion in 1980.

It is now, moreover, a reasonable probability that, under energy investment pressures, and given the conventional policy environment, the Canadian dollar will be pushed over the 90 cent mark in the next few years. This elimination of our only competitive cost advantage will accelerate our finished goods trading deficit to potentially catastrophic proportions. It renders urgent the need to take policy decisions to deliberately maintain the Canadian dollar at its current level or lower. The Hatch Committee, in reporting to the federal government on measures to enhance exports, has commented on the stimulative impact of the lower dollar:

> The enormous decline of the dollar against other major currencies over the past three years has helped turn North America into a much stronger cost-competitive export base. The Canadian dollar of course, has dropped significantly against the U.S. dollar as well. Canadian firms now are much more interested in export markets.[10]

The consequence of a move toward parity has received emphatic comment from other analysts in the private sector:

> To the extent that policy options exist, they should concentrate on maintaining the dollar at existing levels and perhaps not resist, even at the

10

cost of some additional short term inflation, a gradual further decline. Parenthetically, I cannot think of any greater national industrial tragedy, and I emphasize the word tragedy, than an early resurgence of a "strong" Canadian dollar.[11]

It is worth noting in this respect that a principal feature of both Japanese and German economic policy, over the twenty years of their resurgence after World War II, was precisely the management of currency levels to accommodate trading strategy:

> With regard to the Yen, the Japanese government, particularly the Ministry of Finance took the position that the exchange of 360 Yen to the dollar was inviolable from the time it was established in 1949. . . . Maintenance of this single exchange rate was a significant factor in Japan's international trading success. . . . There was a clear willingness to sacrifice a great deal to retain the (artificially low) value of the Yen.[12]

With respect to Germany:

> Price stability and export competitiveness thus becomes the overriding objective of monetary policy, and, in spite of rising export surplus caused by chronic undervaluation of the Deutch Mark, parity maintenance was a dogma . . . . [13]

In the Canadian case, the policy error of maintaining an artificially high dollar has been compounded by the high interest rates which the policy necessitated.

Rapid increases in interest rates have been particularly deleterious to small business, which accounts for a great proportion of job creation. (Small firms are the major source of net new job creation, providing more than 50 per cent of net new private sector jobs between 1971 and 1978)[14] Again, to cite the Japanese economy, where small business is recognized for its dynamic potential, the provision of cheap money is a feature of industrial policy.[15] We in Canada need to consider some form of discretionary policy which will have the effect of reducing the cost of money to small and medium enterprises, (SMEs).

The overriding consideration bearing both upon monetary policy and fiscal strategy is, therefore, their integration into the broader economic goals of trading strength and industrial enhancement. This issue has yet to be resolved at the federal level where institutional change is essential to remove confusion of goals and to put us in step with our trading rivals.

11

2. The Resource Base and Secondary Manufacturing

One of the peculiarities of the Canadian economy is the lack of effective linkages between the resource sector and secondary manufacturing industries. The strength of our primary industries is not used to develop advantages for domestic manufacturing. We see a strong mining industry with no substantial manufacturing of mining machinery; a strong fishing industry with little processing and minimal equipment manufacturing. Contrary to what might be expected by virtue of our resource strength, machinery represents a substantial element ($5 billion) of our trading deficit in manufactured goods.

Canada's situation stands in sharp contrast to that of Sweden, for instance, where strong ties exist between the mining and the mining machinery industry and between both of these and the Swedish government. The consequence is that a strong technology base has been developed in Sweden, as exemplified by ASEA and Bolliden in hard-rock drilling, with products based on that technology being imported into Canada—the largest hard-rock mining market in the world.

The reasons for the lack in Canada of similarly close and fruitful ties between our resource and manufacturing industries are at least fourfold:

(i)   the fact that the Canada/U.S. Defence Sharing Agreement has served to concentrate the Canadian high technology sector primarily on defence-related activities such as aerospace and electronics;

(ii)   the measures taken to enhance the competitive thrust of our extractive industry have included the minimization of tariffs in imported machinery;[16]

(iii) foreign ownership in mining, leading to procurement of equipment from foreign sources;

(iv)   the absence of any policy thrust directed toward using the domestic market base, as represented by the primary sector, to build up Canadian industrial capabilities.

In connection with this last reason, we are now, for instance, on the threshold of a major Canadian resource project, the transportation by marine tanker of liquified natural gas (LNG) from the Eastern Arctic. This LNG tanker program (known currently as the Arctic Pilot Project) is effectively a technology-led revolution in marine transportation, initiated by Canadians as they extend their reach for energy resources to the high Arctic. It will launch year-round marine operations in Arctic waters and will provide some $800 million of ship-building and marine components which could be Canadian in origin.[17] It will also offer technological opportunities well beyond ships and hardware:

> The boost it will give to the electronics industry in developing Arctic navigational aids, and to the engineering of special Arctic port facilities, off-shore and sub-sea structures is important as well. The development of the actual Arctic class ice-breaker is just the tip of the technological iceberg.[18]

The Arctic Pilot Project is precisely the kind of "domestic market base" in the resource sector which should be used to build up Canadian manufacturing industry. The entire infrastructure of this program, its linkages to the development of Labrador and the Atlantic provinces, its long range opportunities in cold-ocean technologies need to be examined, and developmental programs laid down, in order to provide access for Canadians to their own future. Canada has had an oceans policy since 1973.[19] The Arctic Pilot Project is a rare opportunity to put that policy into effect.

A second example, more positive in its results to date, illustrates what can be achieved when the appropriate linkages exist. In the mining equipment sector, Jarvis-Clark Limited of North Bay, Ontario, until recently a small Canadian-owned company[20], created and implemented an entire growth strategy by focussing upon the cooperative development, with Inco Ltd., of underground mining equipment. The success of that cooperation resulted in growth in the annual sales of Jarvis-Clark to some $100 million (1979) and to research and development expenditures in Canada of some $1-2 million per year. The example is regrettably rare, and difficult to repeat, in an industry structure which is dominated by large multinational enterprises and where there is a general absence of adequately sized manufacturing companies among the domestic equipment manufacturers.

According to a CIEP sponsored study of the mining industry:

> There are currently few policy initiatives to encourage change in the structure of the mining equipment supply sector. The large foreign manufacturers dominating the market have little reason to locate new capacity in Canada. Tariffs on imports of machinery and equipment are negligible and provide no incentive to locate "miniature replica" production facilities in subsidiaries here. Additionally, the incremental costs of new capacity in Canada may be higher than for expanding facilities already existing abroad. Neither federal nor provincial governments have specific programs intended to induce foreign suppliers to locate "product mandated" operations in this country.
>
> Domestic (mining machinery) manufacturers and distributors are unlikely to change this situation in the short term . . . domestic manufactur-

ing firms will have to grow rapidly if they are to even retain their market shares in the next decade. Their low research and development capability, together with small relative size, suggests that this hope may well be optimistic.[21]

It is precisely this kind of structural problem that necessitates the application of Positive Adjustment Policies. Trade deficits of mining machinery in the order of $600 million annually, a strong and rising domestic market, but with smaller and smaller participation in it by domestic industry (from 46 per cent to 38 per cent between 1965 and 1975), a weak and fractionated domestic machinery industry—these are the features which justify a positive interventionism designed to stimulate the forces of entrepreneurship and enterprise. Mining machinery manufacturing is a classic case of Canada needing to use her strength and market position in the primary sector to generate more downstream benefits for her economy and her skilled work force. In such an attempt to capitalize on the strength of our resource sector, by building a responsive manufacturing industry, major policy initiatives will be required:

- In the mining machinery sector, the role of CANMET, the federal research activity in mining, could well be substantially increased and supplemented by a responsibility and capability to build up specific developments and produce "alliances" between equipment producers and the mining sector:

  Direct actions include the possible creation of a financing institution similar to the EDC [Export Development Corporation], except that its role would be to fund domestic mineral developments which include significant Canadian equipment content.[22]

- In the ocean resources sector, an industry/trade union task force has called for the creation of COTRA, Canadian Ocean Technology and Research Authority, which would concentrate technological effort and harness and stimulate industrial effort. Such an Authority would greatly facilitate a broad and effective response, for instance, to the demands of the Arctic Pilot (LNG) Project and other ventures.

- Where governments are involved directly in resource development, as in the case of Saskatchewan potash, the provincial government could exercise a direct pressure on the producer to promote associated manufacturing capabilities.

There is a significant potential for action in the resource sector. It represents a natural target for policies aimed at building from strength and at capitalizing on natural advantages.

14

3. Productivity

The large and increasing trade deficit in fully manufactured goods is the measure of the lack of competitiveness of the Canadian manufacturing industry. It reflects our heightened profile as an exporter of raw materials and as a consumer of imported manufactures. That process has to be reversed because we need to employ the skills which we have so expensively developed. The matching of the demand and supply for skilled manpower is the job of industrial policies tailored to major investments in education.

The recovery of competitiveness rests upon a marked improvement in productivity. Enhanced productivity, in turn, depends on specialization, on significant increases in equipment and plant investment, and on rapid advances in technology, as applied both to new products and improved production processes.

Other countries are vigorously attacking this same problem. As manufacturing spreads to lower labour cost countries, productivity through technology becomes the only responsive strategy available. Japan's automation of machine-tool plants, the spread of computer-aided design techniques, advances in robotics, improvements in process controls, the British support of microprocessor application, are all examples of discretionary industrial policies aimed at enhancing productivity and competitiveness. In the United States, similar initiatives are being launched by government in an attempt to play "catch-up ball". Both machine-tool and composite material technology are being accelerated through defence spending, which in the past has proven to be an effective tool for generating technology-based growth in U.S. industry.

The impact of all these policies is changing the shape of modern industry. But the Canadian pace is dramatically slower than its rivals':

> From 1965 to 1972 total business investments (in Canada) grew by 3.7 per cent per annum, whereas from 1973 forward it grew by only 3.5 per cent per annum. Investment in machinery and equipment, on the other hand, showed a much steeper decline from 5.2 per cent per annum in the earlier period to 3 per cent more recently, a 43.0 per cent drop.[23]

Even when manufacturing plant utilization rates have risen, an adequate, corresponding increase in equipment investment has not developed. This, in spite of fast write-off provisions and rich investment tax credits. The policy environment has been too unclear to inspire confidence and encourage adequate levels of investment.

Rationalization, by plant and product-line, will have to be encouraged in order to facilitate the economic application of modern production technologies. Rationalization itself encounters the issue of foreign ownership which in turn illustrates the complexity of industrial policy in Canada. Yet it is one major factor in productivity and must be addressed with greater courage and vigour.

In terms of technology, of "R&D", the Canadian experience has been dismal, and successive federal governments have recognized the severity of the problem. In June 1978 a "catch-up" target of 1.5 per cent of GNP to be expended on research and development was announced, but few formal and specific policy initiatives followed. It has more recently been re-confirmed as an objective by the new government. Yet only in microprocessor and chip technology have significant investments in technology as yet been announced, and even these decisions have not occurred within any framework of priorities. The problem of priorities has to be grasped because the scarce financial resources for productivity improvement must be channelled into those areas where growth is most promising. The concept of choosing priorities and picking winners need not be frightening. In most countries with whom we compete, the selection of priorities for national investment is a commonplace, and potential growth is the criterion for the decision.

In describing Japanese industrial strategy, *The Economist* recently offered the following observation:

> The industries MITI [Ministry of International Trade and Industry] wants to protect do not yet exist, and the old ones it wants to kill are those which we British tax-payers are subsidising to keep going.[24]

Japan has thus selected eight groups of "industries for the future" in which it will concentrate its efforts to achieve highest levels of national productivity.[25] It is essential that Canada emulate this activity. We must select our own priority areas and develop high levels of technological intensity in respect of them. It is widely known that Canadian ownership is highest where technology levels are lowest. *We have secured the commanding heights of the dying industries.* The reverse must be achieved. Substantial, selective technology investment is a key to industrial productivity and to the competitiveness of Canadian industry.

4. New Enterprise in Canada

Of pressing concern in Canada, as well as elsewhere, has been the decline of innovation and the low survival rate of new innovative enterprises. To a great extent the flexibility, productivity and dynamism of the entire industrial system rests upon recurring waves of new small

16

companies seeking new opportunities and creating market niches. The frequency of their birth, their vitality and growth are a measure of the entrepreneurial quality of a nation's industrial activity. All countries recognize this, and Canada has begun to develop its own small business policies.

Nova Scotia's recent *Green Paper* on venture capital articulates the need for innovation:

> Various studies have consistently indicated that independent inventors, including investors, entrepreneurs, and small technologically-based companies, are responsible for more than 2/3 of the important inventions and innovations of this century; and that job creation occurs more rapidly in small/medium innovative, high-technology businesses than in mature organizations.[26]

But we still have much to do to create the most favourable environment for the "fast breeding" of new businesses. Chief among the inhibitors to innovation in Canada are:

- the scarcity and the high cost of venture capital
- a poor risk-reward ratio
- the high cost of operating capital.

With regard to the venture capital gap, the richest provinces are now moving to the subsidization of risk capital to small firms. The newly institutionalized small business development corporations in Ontario and in Quebec, for example, are proving to be successful. Federal incentives to supplement these existing provincial programs would increase their attractiveness and provide a fiscal floor for their adoption in poorer provinces.

As to risk-reward ratio, the introduction of the Capital Gains Tax was an error, and its elimination in manufacturing sectors would remove a powerful disincentive to growth. More generous loss write-off provisions would also be of help. For small and medium-sized businesses interest costs are a major factor; discretionary, favourable interest rates may need to be developed.

Fast-breeding is a regenerating process; the evidence of entrepreneurial success begets its rapid emulation. Successful innovative companies rapidly generate and spin-off newer, equally aggressive businesses.

Based on this phenomenon of spin-off, the Ottawa region is becoming a centre of excellence in advanced electronics technology.

In Japan the small business sector is simultaneously offered a domestic market, stimulated by low cost money, and relieved of overhead cost burdens related to social security. As a consequence, SME's (small and medium enterprises) produce the cost reductions and the new ideas for the larger systems houses and trading companies. The Japanese example illustrates the potential for orchestrated positive adjustment policies to enhance "market forces" and stimulate "enterpreneurship". Industrial policy in Canada must have the same objective. The reward for success will be a re-energizing of economic activity and a substantial increase in job creation.

5. The Management and Ownership of Canadian Industry

An ongoing battle rages over the net benefit to Canada of foreign ownership of our industry. There is no dispute at all about the uniqueness of Canada in terms of the levels of foreign ownership.

TABLE 1.1
Rank Order of Canadian Manufacturing Industries by Degree of Foreign Ownership (Based on Sales in 1974)[27]

	PERCENTAGE FOREIGN OWNED
TOBACCO PRODUCTS	99.8
PETROLEUM AND COAL PRODUCTS	95.7
RUBBER PRODUCTS	90.6
TRANSPORT EQUIPMENT	88.9
CHEMICALS AND CHEMICAL PRODUCTS	81.0
MACHINERY	69.4
ELECTRICAL PRODUCTS	65.6
TEXTILE MILLS	56.1
NON-METALLIC MINERALS	51.7
MISCELLANEOUS MANUFACTURING	47.8
PAPER AND ALLIED INDUSTRIES	42.9
METAL FABRICATION	38.5
PRIMARY METALS	35.8
FOOD	33.3
BEVERAGES	24.9
LEATHER PRODUCTS	22.2
WOOD INDUSTRIES	22.2
KNITTING MILLS	18.6
FURNITURE INDUSTRIES	16.0
CLOTHING INDUSTRIES	12.0
PRINTING AND PUBLISHING INDUSTRIES	11.2
TOTAL	56.3

After twenty years or more of debate there is now a widening consensus that we need to gain a greater control over our own economy. Economic self-determination will benefit both Canada and its Southern neighbour.

The problem itself becomes more tractable when one grasps the fundamentals of the ownership issue. In any rapidly changing condition of economic development the advantages and disadvantages stemming from incoming foreign direct investment also change rapidly. It might have been arguable at one stage, for instance, that foreign ownership was the most effective means of generating short term employment. In this decade, the southward drift of manufacturing activity weakens that already dubious proposition. From the multinational perspective, foreign direct investment was regarded at one time as the most effective method of penetrating foreign markets. Yet, by 1975, such a policy had become increasingly questionable. Professor Robert Gilpin of Princeton argued that "the United States has become over-dependent on foreign investment".[28] The process tended to bleed technology and jobs out of the U.S. economy. MNEs (Multinational Enterprises), for their part, tended to view with greater concern the worries about absolute ownership. As a consequence, the more responsive corporations tend to view joint ventures as being the more attractive vehicle for overseas marketing activities.[29] Indeed, albeit slowly, foreign ownership of Canadian industry is diminishing.[30] The scene has therefore changed considerably. Canadians continue to see the need for an inflow of new technology, but under different ground rules. Multinationals are more flexible in respect of the management of their overseas interests, often being more willing to accord "world product mandates" to their subsidiaries. As the U.S. hard-line position eases, so should our traditional fears of hostility and retaliation recede. Undoubtedly a newer, firmer Canadian position on domestic ownership will be tested, and brought under pressure.

In the international trading game that is to be expected. Yet we must not fail to seek new accommodations. A backbone is as important as a brain. We have many foreign examples to choose from in selecting and deploying our policies relative to ownership.

In Canada, the scene is set for intensifying Canadian ownership of the strategic sectors of industry. The federal government has recognized this, and Mr. Trudeau's speech of February 12, 1980[31] is awaiting amplification and policy content. In surveying its problems and prospects as the industrial heartland, Ontario has developed the same appreciation of the problem. Mr. Grossman, Ontario Minister of Industry and Tourism recently disagreed with a *Globe and Mail* editorial criticizing the Ontario Throne Speech proposal to assist Canadian investors to buy out Canadian operations of foreign owned firms:

> Naturally, the new buy-out assistance program will have to be selective. Government involvement will not be used to prop up unprofitable operations or provide foreign sellers an easy way out of financial difficulties. Applications for assistance will undergo in-depth examination of their market potential, techonological competitiveness and management capabilities. As such, the program will provide the Government with an important tool in assisting Canadians to participate more broadly in good Canadian industrial development and provide our own citizens with the opportunity to compete for facilities that might otherwise, and unnecessarily, be lost abroad.[32]

Policy should now, therefore, aim at the rapid growth of Canadian-owned firms in the fields of energy, transportation, communications, electronics, aviation, petrochemicals and the oceans industries.

The model for emulation is the Canadian steel industry,[33] which stands out in stark contrast not only to other sectors of Canadian industry, but also to other steel industries in the world. Its central characteristics are:

- extremely high technological capability
- good earnings levels
- Canadian private ownership
- competitiveness in price and quality
- heavy capital investment
- it is geared to the domestic market as the base for exports.

In a world steel industry which is mired in problems of high cost levels and over-capacity, this sector of Canadian industry is surviving and growing. One central reason for its success may well be that the management functions reside in this country, making for a highly-focussed and rapid response to changing market conditions.

The formula for success is thus already before us. Policy now needs to aim at creating, in other strategic sectors, Canadian-owned core companies of size and competence, with similar levels of research intensity.

Some progress is being made. Spar Aerospace is being "engineered" into position as the keystone of the Canadian space program. Petro-Canada is being positioned as the national instrument of the oil industry. Canadair and deHavilland afford us a strong base in aviation.

The view is frequently expressed that this "chosen instrument" or "core company" concept involves excessive support by the taxpayer,

20

both by virtue of direct subsidy and by reason of reduced competition. Such a view ignores the demonstrable international trading successes of such policies as pursued by other countries. Close linkages abroad between government and industry have produced fiercely competitive companies in military aircraft and in electronics, companies which control major niches in international markets and which penetrate our own domestic market. The "chosen instrument" is a phenomenon of the modern trading environment; its absence as a policy in Canada has already incurred enormous costs.

The auto industry is a striking example. As a result of the Auto-Pact of 1965 we have rationalized auto production on continental lines, creating an environment in which we are powerless to rectify a rising imbalance of trade ($3.1 billion in 1979), where research and development is centered in the United States, and where domestic managerial authority diminished to the point of non-existence. Free trade in agricultural implements since 1944 has resulted in the transfer of most of this country's production facilities south of the border.

In this environment, the capacity to influence foreign decisions has been weakened. And, by denying ourselves a truly domestic entrepreneurial base, we have more centrally, voluntarily abrogated our capacity to choose and to decide—and this in an industry which dominates the economy of Ontario. One consequence of that self-inflicted malaise, of that loss of autonomy, is that we are repeatedly compelled to provide competitive subsidies of increasing amounts, in a desperate and fruitless attempt to sustain employment through costly, unsuitable guarantees—more and more *danegeld* and less and less power to negotiate.

We will not escape this spiral until we create a viable policy option, a Canadian-controlled vehicle industry with all the technical capabilities and managerial functions it needs to succeed. The costs, estimated to be in the order of $2 billion[34], are not high in comparison with, for instance, projected energy investments. Moreover, such investments in a domestic enterprise may be ultimately less open-ended than those which we now provide to foreign corporations. In each such case of a strategic industry, the issue of ownership has to be grasped because the cost of loss of managerial control is increasingly obvious and unacceptably high.

The object of industrial policy must be to build up selected corporations, or groups of companies, as "core" activities in each sector, using every policy instrument available. It is noteworthy that, as this process develops, the "core" company generates its own infrastructure of technically-responsive suppliers, of spin-off enterprises capitalizing on the same market niche. The diffusion of new technology through the industrial economy, so stifled in a branch-plant economy, is remarkably accelerated when the large core company itself is domestically-owned, and research-intensive in character. Again, the Ottawa-centered complex of electronics companies is vivid evidence of this dynamic process at work.

In oceans industries, as well, it is both desirable and feasible to imitate this same process of growth, based on Canadian ownership, in the Atlantic region. This was indeed an intended outcome of the federal government's oceans policy of 1973.[35] Canadians cannot afford gestation periods of this length.

The policy instruments necessary to achieve this growth of "Canadian-owned and controlled" enterprises in the strategic sectors are available. Federal and provincial purchasing policy is an effective lever, and rationalization incentives are another. If crisis loans of some $200 million can be advanced to an ailing Chrysler, then even more considerable resources are justified in the creation of indigenously owned and managed growth industries.

6. The Optimization of the Canadian Market

In the new world of focussed industrial strategies, trading blocs and cartels, the strength of the Canadian federated state has to be harnessed to the cause of enhancing our international competitive capability. The capacity to exert bargaining power, to "deal" in the most authoritative way across broad areas of economic interest and industrial endeavour, is central to our ability to prosper as a nation, and to contribute to an interdependent global community. In the tougher economic environment of the 1980s, that capacity is crucial.

Yet Ottawa's ability to wield the necessary strength is eroding. The inability or unwillingness, or both, of the federal government to provide leadership in the formulation of industrial strategy has created a vacuum which has attracted a variety of provincial initiatives, aggressively pursued in the provincial interests. These initiatives and policy thrusts reflect a conviction that if, indeed, federation is to generate a surplus not otherwise achievable, that surplus must derive from "a major transformation of the country's economic structure" in which more balanced regional development will be paramount.[36]

As the provincial activities in the area of industrial policy intensify so the Canadian domestic market becomes increasingly "Balkanized" along regional and provincial lines. This is the irony of the double standard. Where Canadians on the one hand disavow non-tariff barriers at their national frontier, they refine and proliferate them at provincial boundaries. Across our national borders flow a rising level of imports, while internally we frustrate attempts by our own manufacturers to build on an aggregated domestic base.

Examples of internal trade barriers are legion. They are strikingly evident in urban transit programs and in the agricultural sector. Professor A. E. Safarian's paper of October 17, 1979, presented at the Ryerson Polytechnical Institute, vividly describes the situation. Provincial government procurement policies, regional development subsidies, energy-use regulations and marketing boards are just some of the instruments deployed to provide preference for suppliers from within the province:

> It is not difficult to enumerate actual or potential problems of this kind in other industries. The communications industry, for example, is one where overlapping jurisdiction and a struggle for power are creating great complications. Try to imagine the complexities of dealing in a national market with 92 provincial and 23 federal laws affecting the storage and transmission of data. . . . [37]

From eggs and chickens to electronics and nuclear engineering, we fractionate domestic markets rather than aggregate them. We compete internally with an energy and enthusiasm which would be admirable if directed abroad.[38] By this process we eliminate the possibility of using our markets as a launching pad for exports. We open ourselves even more to competitive imports from countries which have more wisely developed benefits from their own home markets.

Nevertheless, the day of the central-Canada manufacturing policy may have ended. The traditional notion of specialization based on an industrial heartland and a resource-producing, product-consuming regional hinterland is neither feasible nor desirable. The political economics of Confederation now demand a new pattern of specialization, with industrial capability being linked to the comparative advantage of the region: an oceans industry in the Atlantic region; a petrochemical industry in Alberta; a farming machinery industry in Manitoba.

The new specialization, facilitated by technology and fostered by procurement policies and development incentives, is the basis for a more equitable economic deal in our federated state.

Ignoring the domestic market has been the lacuna in Canadian industrial policy. We have witnessed two decades of vigorous export policies, with little or no attention being paid to the vital home markets. There has been no coherent import replacement policy. Our industrial weakness stems in part from that fact. Policy incentives are long overdue.[39]

If, for instance, the federal government can create a Canadian Commercial Corporation to guarantee foreign governments the export orders sought by Canadian manufacturers, why can it not use the same mechanism to aggregate domestic requirements, say for generators or urban transit systems? If we can promote export consortia, why not import replacement consortia? If we can apply strong, consistent marketing pressure on foreign governments, backed by export financing, why should we not apply the same pressure on our own Crown Corporations, utilities and resource companies backed by import replacement financing?

There is a great need in Canada, not only for export thrusts, but for a high internalization of marketing activity, and for a de-regulation of internal barriers to trade. If industry cannot capture its own domestic base, it will not long survive in foreign markets.

7. New Technology — The Competitive Frontier

The case for the contribution of technology to economic growth has been made.[40] Research intensity is part of the vital equation of economic strength and national sovereignty. In a changing world, paced and powered by technological advance, Canada is losing ground. Reversing that process is critical to the shaping of an adequate future, or even any future, for this country. The strength and competitiveness of Canadian industry will rest upon its capacity to excel technically. "R&D" policy is a means to that end.

On a per capita basis, Canada's "R&D expenditure" performance is slightly better than that of Egypt and is far worse than that of most OECD countries.[41] The problem stems from the structure of Canadian industry, with its high level of foreign ownership and with its preponderance of mature industries, and its paucity of growth companies. Because the problem is structural, the mere force-feeding of R&D funds, in isolation from other policy initiatives, will not be adequate to resolve the problem. One cannot achieve takeoff by putting rocket fuel into a Model-T. The industrial system has to be re-engineered using the entire range of positive adjustment policies available to us.

Given that effort, R&D policies can begin to take hold. In Canada, the cart has been put before the horse. R&D policies have been written, were announced in June 1978[42] (and subsequently re-affirmed), complete with a target of R&D spending which was to achieve a level of 1.5 per cent of GNP by 1983. In order to attain even that goal, which is modest in international terms, an immense effort will be required, and a variety of instruments will need to be utilized.[43]

The main burden will fall upon the private sector. Direct government financial support can only provide the leverage. In the last analysis, the technological enhancement of Canadian industry will

24

occur only when Canadian industry is sufficiently convinced that the Canadian environment is propitious for innovative effort.

In order to help secure that environment and stimulate the necessary momentum, government, in the area of R&D policy, can apply broad measures such as greater tax incentives for the performance of R&D. It should also apply discretionary measures such as selective investments in strategic industries (micro-processors for the electronics industry or process controls for pulp and paper). It should continue to develop and refine corporate guidelines to persuade multinationals to convert their branch plants to entrepreneurial business units, and it should formulate purchasing policies which favour innovative companies. All these policies are already in use or under consideration. The central issue surrounding them is the breadth and scale on which they are applied. Tax incentives are inadequate because they have as yet failed to generate substantial corporate response. Selective investments, such as the "special electronics fund" have been announced but are inadequate in scope and hesitantly applied.

Corporate guidelines have been in existence for several years, but the degree of moral suasion, or the incentives or penalties, have clearly not been sufficient, in the main, to encourage multinational enterprises to allocate research and development activities to their Canadian subsidiaries, or to channel R&D funds into the Canadian economy. It is interesting in this connection to note Norway's experience relative to the off-shore oil industry. When the decision is taken to award oil concessions to corporations committed to industrial development in Norway, and when the oil corporations are advised that investment in technology is a key aspect of industrial development, the result is a flow of funds into the national R&D base which is helping to rejuvenate the industrial economy of Norway. The examples are there if Canadian policy-makers wish to learn. If we were to apply the same policy to our own on-shore and off-shore oil industry, the results might prove to be equally stimulating.

Purchasing policy is developing, but slowly. In this last connection, for instance, the huge potential impact of the Crown Corporations, such as the CBC, and Petro-Canada, has not been generated because the role of these institutions as instruments of a national industrial policy is not yet fully appreciated. The defence purchases of capital equipment may total $30 billion over the next decade, and many of these purchases are high in technology content. Yet there is no effective application of these purchases to the enhancement of industry's technical capacity. This must be accounted one of the significant failures of our R&D policy. In the main, our purchasing policies and practices have done more to serve foreign technology than our own.

There are three broad areas in which our R&D efforts need to be harnessed:

- We must take action to participate in the van of the newer, broader fronts of basic research which will determine the direction and pace of future growth. The micro-processor, chip technology revolution is one such front. We are already threatened with being submerged by the tidal wave of chip technology from abroad and we have to find means to ride the crest. That case has been made. The Canadian response to date is not adequate by any standards.

- A second such advanced research front is rapidly emerging, equally pervasive, and perhaps even more significant in terms of its own potential impact on Canadian industry and the Canadian economy. Microbiology and gene manipulation are new frontiers whose breadth and depth are only just beginning to be discerned. The "clone" is as revolutionary as the transistor. The livestock, agricultural and petrochemical industries are on the threshold of profound change. In genetics research Canada is half a decade behind. Our research is scattered and underfunded. The linkages between university genetics research capability and industry are already being forged in the United Kingdom and the U.S., but are almost non-existent in Canada. It is vital that we now secure a research bridgehead in genetics—a concentration of funding and scientific excellence, a concerted industrial expertise and commercialization process—from all of which new technology and strength may flow. Strategic research of this kind is the foundation of our technological future.

- As a second broad R&D strategy, the technological assault on manufacturing processes and methods has to be launched, in order to secure the productivity advances central to competitive performance. Computer-aided design, microprocessors for batch-switching, robotics for medium-scale production represent the revolution now in progress. The diffusion of these technologies throughout Canadian industry has to be orchestrated.

- Supplementing this "strategic" research policy, large scale funding support is needed for specific technological activities geared to perceived social needs and to national demand: alternative energy systems; pollution abatement; ocean-related equipment; and resource project instrumentation. Technology policy must stress application and be geared to known demand.

Where R&D policy has in the past ignored the realities of the marketplace it has failed dramatically. Where the market niche has been correctly discerned, R&D policy has succeeded. In the aerospace sector both the Dash-7 and the Challenger are testimonies to that fact. It is undeniable that, in pursuit of the above three research and development strategies, Canada will need to continue to supplement its own intensified efforts with imported know-how. Indeed, there is every reason to believe that our demands will intensify. Canada cannot, and should not, strive for total self-sufficiency. Yet the form in which such technology arrives, and the flexibility with which it can subsequently be deployed, is increasingly important. In this context, technological joint ventures between foreign and domestic companies are preferable to know-how importation through direct foreign investment. Much greater attention must be paid to acquiring, in areas of special interest such as tar sands and heavy oils, basic research knowledge rather than merely production technology. It is essential that we build on what we get, and freely exploit what we build.

It should be emphasized also that, in a world where technology has become the new currency of international competition, Canada must contribute more of its own technology to the global knowledge pool. We must have the chips to play in the game. It is already evident in military R&D that the country with nothing to offer is being closed out of the international exchange of advanced technology. Canada must pay its technology "share" if it is to play a responsible role and reap an adequate benefit.

The upgrading and acceleration of our national technological effort will involve enormous effort and cost. Failure to proceed will be even more costly. It is nevertheless ironic that when $50 million is scraped together for the national push in electronics, $200 million is being advanced for the temporary relief of Chrysler. The proper ordering of our priorities is long overdue.

It is worth emphasizing that R&D policy is not an end in itself. The achievement of higher research intensity is not its own reward. Although admirable and well-motivated, recent federal policy announcements bearing on science policy place the cart before the horse. It is a strong industry which will deploy R&D incentives, and not R&D incentives which will create strong industry. Ownership and rationalization policies must be developed in order to ensure that maximum national benefits are derived from science policy. It is the essence of strategy that a complete range of policies be adopted and implemented in pursuit of a specific goal.

The system architecture of an industrial strategy for Canada, which has been reviewed, has as its clear objective the revitalization of the Canadian manufacturing industry in terms of its size, strength, productivity, vitality and competitiveness. The fate of the Canadian economy rests upon the success of that endeavour. We are dealing with *a viable* strategy for Canada, and we must approach it, in terms of both substance and management, with all the coherence and concentration that "strategy" implies.

The Management of Industrial Strategy

Whatever else may be involved in the industrial policy prescriptions for an ailing Canadian economy, the need for a greater sophistication of approach is paramount. A world of rapid change and of increasingly imperfect markets demands it. With a comparatively open economy, Canada must adopt, and learn to manage, a much more comprehensive industrial strategy than has been previously considered. There can be no return to simplicity. There is no big brother to rely on. There is only an increasingly complex and competitive world to which, as an independent nation, we must find an increasingly complex and effective response.

As a trading nation we have no choice but to play, and win, in the world arena. As an industrial nation we have no choice but to pursue those "positive adjustment policies" which will develop our entrepreneurial strength and our free-market capabilities.

On balance, the management of industrial and trading policy has increased, rather than decreased, as a result of the recently completed Tokyo Round of GATT. To compensate for projected real or illusory tariff reductions the member nations are erecting policies based on their own strategic interests. The U.S. itself, more alert and more aware than ever before of the competitive threat from abroad, is developing a regulatory system responsive to its own vital needs.

In a recent speech to the Conference Board in Canada, Mr. Rodney de C. Grey, the former head of the Canadian delegation to the Multinational Trade Negotiations in Geneva, described this phenomenon and presented a Canadian prescription:

> Looking at this legislation (the United States Trade Agreement Act of 1979) and trying to assess the actions of the whole negotiations, and looking at our prospects—it is important to understand that, oratory aside, the United States has not, as a result of the MTN, lowered its barriers to imports. What has happened is that, in parallel with agreeing to reduce certain tariff rates in the future, the United States has refined and articulated its various legal mechanisms for dealing with import competition . . .
> It is certainly not clear that the new system—or better, the strengthened, redesigned, highly articulated, regulatory system—will be less restrictive of imports into the United States than was the pre-Kennedy round system. . . . We have to come to terms with a new regulatory trade policy.

That means, first, understanding it. It also means quite inevitably, adapting, and adopting it into our own framework of law.[44]

Regulatory trade policies, complex countervailing procedures, detailed bi-lateral negotiations and, internally, the erection of a wide range of macro and micro industrial policies, are the essence of the new regime which both the public and the private sector have jointly to manage. The strain and resources involved will be substantial. The need for such an overall strategy to be based on broad intersectoral agreement will add to the challenge. Somehow, a uniquely Canadian management pattern has to emerge, neither as *dirigiste* as the French model, nor as unstructured as our current approach.

At the onset, Canadians have to accept that, somewhat paradoxically, in order to build a strong market economy from a weak industrial base, the role of government will be significant. Indeed, a problem in Canada, frequently distorted in perspective, is not that we have too strong a government, but that we have too weak a private sector. Building up the latter is more appropriate than dismantling the policies of the former.

Discerning Canadian business leaders are beginning to appreciate the role and responsibility of government in the context of industrial strategy. Rowland Frazee, Chief Executive of the Royal Bank, commented on this point in a recent interview:

> "I'm not scared of an industrial strategy", Frazee says. "We in the Royal Bank do strategic planning. Why shouldn't the government do strategic planning?" He notes that the bank has picked its winners for the 1980s— industries such as communications, resources and agriculture, for example —and sees no reason why government can't pick winners as well.[45]

Thus, the notion of strategic planning as a managerial task of government is beginning to be accepted. So also is the idea of specialization— of selecting and picking winners. This is true even in the heartland of the free market system, the United States, where government is establishing, for instance, non-profit generic technology centres which will be "targeted" on a technology that is involved in the processes of several industrial sectors, and has the potential for significant technological upgrading.

Government's role in industrial policy should be strong, and it should be welcome. We have a right to expect that its managerial contribution be flexible, innovative and collaborative.

In terms of the need for flexibility, it is undeniable that, in Canada, the formulation and implementation of industrial policy are stifled

29

under the sheer weight and inertia of the federal department responsible for that mission. It is, moreover, weakened because a sufficiently authoritative focal point for all aspects of industrial strategy has yet to be established at Cabinet level. These two critical weaknesses serve to bureaucratize and ossify, rather than to energize and stimulate. There is no reason why this should be so. Flexibility is not the antithesis of accountability, and considerable attention to achieving more momentum and focus in the Ottawa bureaucracy is merited.

Specifically, there is, and has been for some time, a strong case for the separation of Industry from the Department of Trade and Commerce. A Department of Industry was established in 1963, but was merged with the Department of Trade and Commerce in 1968 because it was felt that, "trade promotion [was] the nearest thing to industrial policy that trading nations would wish to undertake."[46]

The double mandate of this Department has frequently and consistently weakened its industrial policy thrust. It has also resulted in a size and inertia which has frustrated industry and confounded flexible and responsive decision-making.

Until such a change occurs, import containment policy will never emerge as a complementary thrust to export promotion, and a further succession of ministers will be pressured irresistibly into reacting more and thinking less. The recent tripartite division of the departmental ministers, with industrial policy, small business and trade responsibilities, does help. But even that fails to substantially reduce the partial paralysis generated by one massive institution.

Institutional innovation is already in evidence in other areas. The creation of Petro-Canada at the federal level and AOSTRA (Alberta Oil Sands Technology and Research Authority)[47] represent very promising attempts to focus decision-making in strategically important areas of the economy. The extension of this institutional innovation to the space program,[48] and to the oceans program,[49] will be welcome. In the critical area of linking university research resources to industry, the "Action concertée" program in Quebec[50] is an example of what can be achieved in Canada. This particular linkage is notoriously weak and needs more attention and support at the provincial, as well as the federal level. Finally, the SBDCs (small business development corporations) are innovative Canadian institutions which hold great promise for smaller Canadian businesses.

Collaboration presages the achievement of the wide consensus essential to a national industrial strategy. In a highly perceptive article published in 1978, Albert T. Sommers of the U.S. Conference Board wrote:

Finally, if there is a fundamental need ... for bridges across the divide that separates government and its end from business and its means, joint investment, joint consultation, even joint educational efforts, can help break down the stereotypes that limit cooperation on both sides. It is hard to think of anything that would help more to re-enlist the American public in active allegiance to its employers and its government than evidence that the two can subscribe together to a vision of the American future.[51]

In Canada, following the MacLaren Report[52], a great deal has been done to involve industry and labour in the process of industrial policy formulation. The Hatch Committee and the Major Project Task Force are similarly progressive. With this trend toward greater consulation, "who plays God" is becoming an outdated objection to coherent action.

In any review of the management of an industrial strategy for Canada, it becomes evident that the leadership demands upon the federal government are enormous. The growing sophistication of the international bargaining process, the need for sponsoring greater intersectoral collaboration at home, the need for more institutional innovation, and for more flexible policy response all imply a highly "centralist" approach which is the antithesis of the decentralizing influences at work in our federal system. Fears of undue centralism have provoked serious questions as to whether an industrial strategy for Canada can be adopted and, if adopted, whether it could be successfully implemented. To many, the absence of a strong central mechanism defies the application of a coherent strategy. In this connection, Dr. Michael Jenkin has observed that,

When one compares the institutional and administrative situation in Europe and Japan with that in this country, it is apparent that Canada displays few of the features which have facilitated industrial development strategy abroad.[53]

He adds, with Simeon, that "there is now no single authority that can dominate public policy with respect to industry.[54]

Yet the potential federal role and influence in the formulation and direction of an industrial strategy for Canada is still strong and multifaceted. Federal financial participation in major capital projects is likely to become more frequent as capital costs increase. The creation of export marketing agencies will be undertaken by the federal government. The influence of federal government and Crown Corporation purchasing will increase; the capacity and willingness to deal with multinational enterprises will intensify; inter-government bargaining in sectored areas of industrial activity may well represent a major opportunity for advance.[55]

Canadians would be unwise, in short, to abandon the search for an industrial strategy because of any assumed inherent incapacity to manage such a strategy. When the need is so apparent and the cost of vacillation so great, an innovative managerial response becomes increasingly feasible and desirable.

Industrial Strategy—Examples in the Domestic Sector

In order to appreciate the different results that could be obtained given coherent application over any sustained period of time, consider the application of industrial strategy to particular industrial sectors:

Defence

Over the last twenty years, Canada has militarily (if not organizationally) enjoyed some stability in its commitments to NATO and NORAD and to peace-keeping activities. Industrially, we have lived under the Defence Production Sharing Agreement with the United States, initially with some success, and latterly with a growing negative imbalance of trade. A succession of foreign weapon systems have been built over the period, and some $30 billion of further capital expenditures are planned by the Department of National Defence over the present decade.

In many countries, military expenditures are traditionally an important instrument of industrial policy. They are used to maintain a minimum level of preparedness in the event of war; they are used to develop and enhance strategic sectors of the industrial economy such as aerospace and electronics; they furnish some support for more mature industries such as textiles and clothing. Most importantly, perhaps, military programs are used to achieve a major injection of advanced research and development activity into the industrial base. In this connection, massive U.S. defence spending after World War II was a major contributor to the rapid technological and productivity advances achieved by American industry in the 1950s and beyond. Sweden and France are notable examples of the same pattern of activity.

In Canada, the cancellation of the Arrow program in 1959 ended any sustained attempt to link military procurement to the achievement of Canadian industrial strength and excellence. The Defence Sharing

Agreement with the United States promised us production work on the implicit understanding that Canada would never again attempt to develop major systems. As our system capacity consequently diminished, our choices narrowed to those already designed and produced foreign aircraft we could afford, and as to how much build-to-print production we might generate in Canada from those purchases. The Defence Sharing Agreement initially produced a trade surplus, largely due to Viet Nam demand. This then moved into deficit as all major procurements, all systems requirements, all critical technology, inexorably poured in from abroad. Research and development activities in Canada declined and reflected the lower tempo and reduced momentum of Canadian industry. An internal report of the Department of National Defence observed, ruefully yet succinctly, that Canadian manufacturing was weak, and was weakest where the technological requirement was highest.

Loss of systems capability, restriction of choices, growing technological dependency, limited research activity and the emergence of the inevitable quantitative and qualitative deficits in trade make the defence sector parallel the weakness implicit in the Auto Pact.

The spiral can be broken. The defence programs can be deployed as a key component of a Canadian industrial strategy. "National Defence" has to accept that industrial health and economic strength are as important in guaranteeing national security as the weaponry which is purchased. Indeed, in a period of increasing technological protectionism, the Canadian military role itself may require the support of a technically stronger and more stable industrial base:

- The appropriate strategy will be to use defence spending to intensify research and development in Canada, to build up Canadian-owned industry, and to build up a systems capability that in turn influences sources of production. These objectives must be imposed and planned across the entire span of defence purchasing, and over a decade or more of activity. The new fighter aircraft, the emerging patrol frigate, the new air traffic control systems must be used, with consensus planning and foresight, to increase Canadian systems competence and to generate the flow of new Canadian products. No military program of any substance should be approved which does not clearly contribute to these industrial goals.

- Secondly, defence research and development funds should be linked to long term procurement planning, and fed to the Canadian-owned technical companies, so as to position them to win increasingly larger amounts of the major purchases as they develop. Thus, over a decade, specific, growing, technologically advanced Canadian companies will emerge, with particular types of expertise, and with the muscle necessary to compete in world markets.

- Thirdly, in defence purchasing, a formula should be developed to provide the selected supplying companies with a percentage of negotiated price to be devoted to "free research", thus broadening the corporate capacity to increase research intensity and enhance market opportunity. Canada must build on strength.

- Finally, the defence production sharing agreement should be renegotiated in order to allow for the allocation of selected major systems activity to Canada. It is neither acceptable nor rewarding that Canada should relegate itself to a "build-to-print" status. If we agree that the United States should develop and design the fighter aircraft which we plan to use, we should also insist that the other North American requirements for mutually needed aircraft be allocated to Canada under the agreement. Canada must get back into systems activity, because that level implies managerial autonomy, technical responsibility and market opportunities.

Such a strategy for defence, where it is linked to industrial growth, is commonplace outside Canada. It is feasible. It is vital. This is not, of course, to argue for higher levels of defence expenditure. But it does argue that, in deciding to commit such expenditures, their content should be shaped by the industrial benefits which could accrue to the nation. To a considerable extent, the military roles accepted by some countries reflect their industrial and economic interests. Like other countries, Canada can develop advantage from necessity. Although our defence base is narrow, and far from self-sufficient, it is both rational and crucial that we seek military roles, systems, responsibilities and research missions which strengthen our industrial economy.

Off-Shore Oil and Gas

The same strategic approach as that applied to defence could readily be developed, given the will-power, to the off-shore oil and gas area of the Canadian resource sector. This is a useful example because the off-shore programs are in their infancy and because we have a vivid and successful precedent in Norway, whose programs and difficulties are quite similar.

The challenge of producing oil from 200-1000 metre depths in the cold ocean environment involves massive technical difficulties and, therefore, significant opportunity. In Norway, the awarding of drilling concessions is linked by the Norwegian government to the propensity of the applicant (the oil company) to subscribe to Norwegian industrial benefit and, in particular, to contribute to Norwegian research and development activity.

One result of that friendly suasion is a growing level of technical demand on Norwegian industry (for instance, in electronics), a growing linkage between the resource and secondary manufacturing sectors, a closer relationship between university research and user applications and a rising level of "exportable" competence in the domestic industry.

Canada must emulate this example. The necessary off-shore development regulations are in place, if we have the wit to use them. A combination of federal/provincial suasion, the creation of a COTRA (Canadian Ocean Technology Research Authority) and other such focussing activities would act as a seed-bed for the industry which could be built around the burgeoning off-shore oil fields. If we do not develop this industry we will lose all the attendant opportunities. In five years, we may once again have to import foreign technology.

These two examples, defence and off-shore oil, show what can, and must, be done to rebuild our industrial strength. All the cardinal principles of industrial strategy are present: Canadian ownership; technological intensity; productivity enhancement; the linking of primary and secondary sectors; the support of Canadian entrepreneurial activity. This type of approach can be repeated in, and adapted to, sector after sector, under the overall architecture of a coherent industrial strategy.

Conclusion

Involving as it does the restructuring and revitalizing of Canadian industry, the development and implementation of an industrial strategy is a matter of one to two decades, a period which contrasts sharply with the electoral time-frames within which so many political decisions are made. Hence the need for a substantial consensus as to its outlines and guiding principles; hence the perceived significant difficulties in applying "a strategy".

Yet the attempt to achieve and maintain a consensus, to realize a broad and coherent industrial strategy for Canada, is vital for at least three major reasons:

- In the new reality of an increasingly competitive world, Canada is falling behind. In spite of the policy tools and natural strengths available to us, we are failing because of the absence of clear goals and priorities, and because of the lack of effective orchestration of policy. It is a race which we cannot afford to lose.

- The consequence of the absence of strategy is a restriction of choice and an entrapment in short term and unpalatable options. The Chrysler decision in the auto sector and the new fighter aircraft decision in defence, typify the result of strategic inactivity. In this environment almost all the choices are poor ones.
- The essence of an industrial strategy for Canada is that it must strengthen the market system and enhance the nation's entrepreneurial capacity. The private sector must be strengthened through a wide variety of positive adjustment policies. Unless that is done, the inevitable succession of crises and failures will dictate the larger role of government and remorseless stifling of forces central to our economic well-being and our political sovereignty.

Canada must, in order to survive, accept the transition to reality. The process will be lengthy, painful and costly—but not as costly as would a refusal to face facts. The search for consensus will be inordinately difficult—but not as difficult as survival under current polarizations. In a period of rapid change the imperatives are that we clearly understand the world we live in, we exert and maintain more control over our own environment, and we accept responsibility for our own choices. The shaping of an exciting and challenging new future, by Canadians, now lies within the grasp of Canadians.

Appendix

The OECD "Orientations"

The following is an extract from the Communiqué adopted by the OECD Ministerial Meeting in June 1978.* It is taken from the Communiqué's Annex II, entitled "Policies for Adjustment: Some General Orientations."

Industrial Policy

In responding to requests for help from enterprises in the industrial sector in financial difficulty, it should be recognized that under normal conditions there is usually a presumption against selective action to assist loss-making activities, in favor of more general measures. Where the difficulties being encountered are mainly cyclical, they will normally be best handled by measures to facilitate access to external sources of finance and to raise demand and improve profitability in the economy as a whole. Even where the difficulties are more deep-seated, reflecting unanticipated adverse trends in demand or competition from other sources of supply, special intervention will normally only be justified if the economic or social costs of the necessary adjustments are likely to be unacceptably high in the short run, and cannot be adequately handled through existing policies to ease the burdens of adjustment. Thus, cases where specific action to protect or support individual sectors or companies in financial difficulty can be justified, and are likely to be successful, should be relatively rare.

*OECD Communiqué A(78)23 of 15 June 1978.

37

Where, nevertheless, governments find it necessary to intervene, experience has shown the importance of the following criteria:

(i)   Action should be temporary and should, wherever possible, be reduced progressively according to a prearranged timetable.

(ii)   Such action should be integrally linked to the implementation of plans to phase out obsolete capacity and reestablish financially viable entities, without, however, seeking to raise prices above levels providing an adequate return to efficient producers.

(iii)   The cost should be made as evident as possible to decision-makers and the public at large. Careful attention should be paid to the cost to consumers of action which raises prices, to the cost to taxpayers and to the effects of subsidized competition on employment elsewhere.

(iv)   Where public funds are being injected into the private sector, it is desirable that private risk capital should be involved.

(v)   Assistance given on a company-by-company basis should be framed so as to provide an incentive for improved management practices, notably by ensuring sufficient domestic and international competition.

(vi)   Where the primary objective is to support employment in particular regions or towns, consideration should be given to action that can benefit any eligible company in the area concerned, rather than only those in financial difficulty.

(vii)   While recognizing that governments must pay due regard to the interests of national security, care should be taken to see that arguments based on considerations of self-sufficiency should not be misused to justify measures for protection and support.

To varying degrees, OECD governments have tried to follow industrial policies aimed at "picking the winners." Experience shows, however, that this is far from easy, particularly for industrial countries at the frontiers of technological progress and changing patterns of consumption, and possessing roughly similar factor endowments and management skills.

There are, however, directions in which, according to country circumstances, policies based on rational economic criteria may seek to supplement market forces in promoting desirable developments. For example:

(i)   There are certain areas where markets are unlikely adequately to reflect and anticipate future economic and social needs. This applies, for example, to research and development and investment in producing and saving energy; to improvements in environmental quality, health care, urban infrastructure, etc.

(ii)   Recent difficulties have caused many companies to reduce long-term research in advanced technologies involving large investments, in favor of research to meet more immediate requirements. Governments should, therefore, ensure that adequate incentives for long-term research and development exist.

(iii)   Since much technological progress and response to changed demands has come from small and medium-sized companies, there is a good case for strengthening policies designed to ensure that they have adequate access to venture capital and incentives and opportunities to innovate, specialize and modernize.

Notes

[1] John Kenneth Galbraith, *Economics and the Public Purpose* (New York, New American Library, 1975), p. xi.

[2] Jannifer Lewington, "Buy America Policy Shuts out Canadians", *Financial Times* (October 29, 1979), p. 17.

[3] "Government-backed Europeans Tough Competition for Ontario Firms" *Toronto Star*, (January 11, 1980).

[4] Trilateral Commission, "Policies for Adjustment: Some General Considerations", in Trilateral Task Force on Industrial Policy, *Industrial Policy and the International Economy*, Report (New York University Press, 1979) pp. 71, 72.

[5] Trilateral Commission. *Industrial Policy and the International Economy, op. cit.*

[6] *Ibid.*, p.67.

[7] Sidney Harman, "For an America Inc.," *Newsweek* (March 12, 1979), p. 21.

[8] Arthur Donner and Douglas D. Peters, *The Monetarist Counter-Revolution* (Ottawa, Canadian Institute for Economic Policy, 1979), pp. 23-37.

[9] Canada, Statistics Canada, *Summary of External Trade* (Ottawa, December 1979), Tables X-1 and M-1.

[10] Canada, Ministry of Industry, Trade and Commerce. Export Promotion Review Committee (Hatch Committee), "Strengthening Canada Abroad", Final Report (Ottawa, November 20, 1979), p. 13.

[11] J. J. Singer, "Practical Approaches to Exchange Rate Policies in our Current Account Deficit; A Need for Action", *Occasional Paper No. 1* (Ottawa, Canadian Institute for Economic Policy, 1979), p. 16.

[12] J. J. Pempel, "Japanese Foreign Economic Policy: The Domestic Bases for International Behaviour" in Peter Katzenstein, ed., *Between Power and Plenty* (Madison, University of Wisconsin Press, 1977), p. 186.

[13] Michael Kreile, "West Germany: The Dynamics of Expansion" in Katzenstein, *ibid.*, pp. 193, 194.

[14] Toronto Stock Exchange, *Taking Stock: Investment and Enterprise into the 1980s* (Toronto, September 1979), p. 11.

[15] Trilateral Commission, *op. cit.*, p. 16.

[16] Canada, Ministry of Industry, Trade and Commerce, "Canadian Machinery Industry Sector Task Force", *Report* (Ottawa June 1978), pp. 8-9.

[17] Canadian Arctic Resource Committee (CARC), "The Arctic Pilot Project, Submission to the Environment Assessment and Review Process" (Ottawa, March 1980), p. 55.

[18] *Ibid.*

[19] Canada, Ministry of State for Science and Technology, "New Oceans Policy", News Release (Ottawa, July 12, 1973).

[20] In connection with this example, it is interesting to note that Jarvis-Clark has converted from Canadian to foreign ownership, which raises other

40

industrial policy issues. Was foreign ownership the only method available to finance growth? Should the powers of FIRA be strengthened to protect Canadian ownership in strategic sectors? If federal financing has been involved in the growth of a Canadian company, what onus on maintaining domestic ownership, or on securing a recovery of such assistance, rest with the government? Is the Canadian equity market an insufficiently attractive alternative to foreign investment?

21 Peter Richardson, *et. al.*, *Mining's Missing Linkages* (unpublished report), Canadian Institute for Economic Policy, p. 91.

22 *Ibid.*, p. 119

23 *Taking Stock, op. cit*, p. 8.

24 Norman Macrae, "Must Japan Slow?", *The Economist*, (February 23, 1980), p. 28.

25 *Ibid.*, pp. 28, 33.

26 Nova Scotia Task Force on Venture Capital, "Toward Venture Capital in Nova Scotia", prepared for Minister of Development, July 1979; in *Taking Stock, op. cit.*, p. 11.

27 Canada, Science Council of Canada, "Toward International Technological Interdependence: Annual Statement of the Chairman", Dr. Josef Kates, in *Annual Report, 1977-78*, p. 29.

28 Robert Gilpin, "An Alternative Strategy to Foreign Investment", *Challenge* (November-December 1975).

29 P. G. Van DerSpeck, "The Multinational Firm in a Drastically Changed World." *The Business Quarterly* (Spring 1975), pp. 22-29.

30 Canada, Statistics Canada, *Corporation and Labour Unions Returns Act 1977* (Catalogue No. 61-210).

31 "Trudeau, Industry Plan: Play our Energy Card", *Toronto Star* (February 13, 1980), p. A10.

32 Larry Grossman, "Buy-Out Plan Advances Canadian Participation", Letter to the Editor, *Globe and Mail* (April 10, 1979).

33 Canada, Ministry of Industry, Trade and Commerce, "The Canadian Primary Iron and Steel Industry", *Report of the Sector Task Force*, A. V. Orr, Chairman (Ottawa, December 1978), p. 5 of Sector Profile.

34 Simon Reisman, "The Canadian Automotive Industry"; *Commission of Inquiry into the Automotive Industry* (Ottawa, Department of Industry, Trade and Commerce, October 1978), pp 221-222.

35 Canada, Ministry of State for Science and Technology, "New Oceans Policy", News Release (Ottawa, July 12, 1973).

36 Judith Maxwell and Caroline Pestieau, *Economic Realities of Contemporary Confederation* (Montreal, C. D. Howe Research Institute. March 1980), p. 25.

37 A. E. Safarian, "Ten Markets or One?; Regional Barriers to Economic Activity in Canada", Paper presented at Ryerson Polytechnical Institute (Toronto, October 17, 1979), p.4.

38 Maxwell and Pestieau, *op. cit.*, p. 85.

39 John Cornwall, *Modern Capitalism: Its Growth and Transformation* (London, Martin Robertson, 1977), pp. 193-4.

40 E. F. Denison, "Accounting for U.S. Economic Growth 1929-1969", Brookings Institution, Washington D.C., 1974). His econometric studies showed

that over the period 1929-1969 technological innovation was responsible for 85 per cent of the overall productivity increase, which in turn accounted for 45 per cent of U.S. economic growth during these 40 years.

Cf. M. Boretsky, "Consensus about the present American position in International Trade", NAE Symposium on Technology and Trade (Washington, D.C. October 1970); "Trends in U.S. Technology; a Political Economist's View", *American Scientist* (January 1975); "U.S. Technology Trends and Political Issues", *Monograph No. 17* (George Washington University, October 1974). He has shown, among other things, that technology intensive manufacturing industry outperformed other manufacturing in the following respect: 45 per cent faster growth in output; 80 per cent high growth in employment; 38 per cent higher growth in productivity; 44 per cent lower increase in price per unit output; 48 per cent higher growth in exports (1962-71), in Science Council, *Annual Report, 1977-78*, p. 31.

[41] *Taking Stock, op, cit.,* p. 7.

[42] Canada, Ministry of State for Science and Technology, "Support for Industrial Research" by Judd Buchanan, Press Release (Ottawa, June 1, 1978).

[43] Canada, Ministry of State for Science and Technology, "R&D in Canada", Ad hoc Advisory Committee to the Minister of State for Science and Technology (Ottawa, August 1979), p. 9.

[44] Rodney de C. Grey, "Challenge of the Tokyo Round", Conference Board in Canada, Notes for a speech (Ottawa, September 26, 1979), pp. 10, 15, 16, 17.

[45] David Crane, "This Man Stumps the Country Talking Economics, Not Politics", *Toronto Star* (January 26, 1980).

[46] Richard French, *How Ottawa Decides: Planning and Industrial Policy-Making 1968-80*(Ottawa, Canadian Institute for Economic Policy, 1980), p. 110.

[47] In creating the Alberta Oil Sands Technology and Research Authority, Premier Lougheed stated the major responsibility of the Authority is to develop the technology needed to establish a commercial *in-situ* method of oil sands recovery in Alberta at the earliest possible date.
Alberta Oil Sands Technology and Research Authority, *Annual Report* (March 31, 1977), p.7.

[48] J. J. Shepherd, "Canada's Pressing Need for a National Space Agency", *Globe and Mail* (April 3, 1980), p. 7.

[49] Canada, Department of Industry, Trade and Commerce, Sector Task Force (Chairman T. Nickerson), "The Canadian Ocean Industry Report" (Ottawa), p. 4.

[50] Noranda Research Centre "Action Concertée, a Powerful Tool for Successful R&D", by W. H. Gauvin (Pointe Claire, November 1978).

[51] Albert T. Sommers, "A Collision of Ethics and Economics", Conference Board, *Across the Board,* (New York July 1978).

[52] Canada, Ministry of Industry, Trade and Commerce, Task Force on Business-Government Interface, "How to Improve Business-Government Relations in Canada", *Report* (Ottawa, September 1976).

[53] Michael Jenkin, "The Prospects for a New National Policy" *Journal of Canadian Studies* 14, No. 3 (Fall, 1979), p. 128.

[54] *Ibid.,* p. 129.

[55] *Ibid.,* p. 135.

42